Contents

Light all around

LIGHT THAT COMES DIRECTLY from the Sun lights up our Earth. Without it there would be no life here at all. Things which make light, like the Sun, are called sources of light. Some light comes directly from the source, some is reflected, some is natural and some is artificial.

Be amazed

Amaze yourself and your friends by doing the exciting experiments in this book. You will find out lots of interesting facts about light – where it comes from, what it can do, how it helps us to see and why we need it to live.

Look closely

Scientists always ask lots of questions and observe carefully. Look closely to see what is happening. Don't be upset if your predictions do not always turn out to be correct, as scientists (and that includes you!) learn a lot from unexpected results.

Be careful

Always make sure an adult knows that you are doing an experiment. Ask for help if you need to use sharp tools or glass. Never look straight at the sun as it can damage your eyes. And don't touch light sources such as bright bulbs or lit candles as they can burn you. Follow the step-by-step instructions carefully and remember – be a safe scientist!

Look at these pictures and try to see what the sources of the light are. Can you tell which light sources are natural and which are made by people? See which pictures show light coming straight from the source and which pictures show light which is reflected. Try and imagine a world without either sunlight or light made by electricity. The following experiments will show you how important light is in our daily lives.

Bright light!

WHERE DOES LIGHT COME FROM? It can come from all kinds of different sources. Light bulbs are important sources of light in our everyday lives. Electricity is used to make bulbs light up. Find out how in the following experiment.

SAFETY. The amount of electricity you will use in this experiment is tiny so it is safe to do. However, the amount that comes from mains electricity (used to light lamps at home for example) is much greater, so NEVER experiment or play with anything using mains electricity.

✔ you will need
- ✔ 2 lengths of single strand wire (approx. 15 cm long)
- ✔ a torch bulb
- ✔ a bulb holder
- ✔ insulating tape
- ✔ a 1.5v battery
- ✔ a battery holder
- ✔ a screwdriver

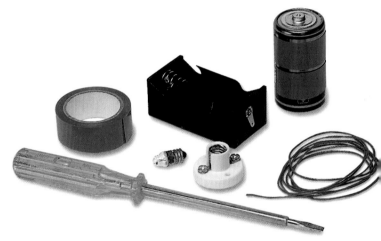

1 Get an adult to cut the plastic covering off the ends of each piece of wire.

2 Screw the bulb into the bulb holder.

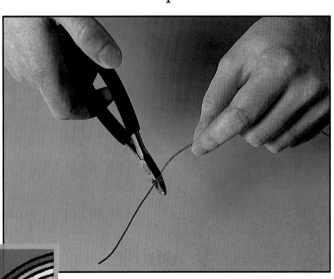

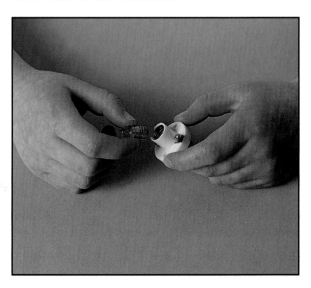

3 With the screwdriver, attach one end of each piece of wire onto the bulb holder.

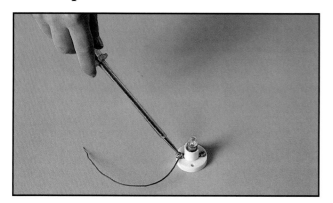

4 Using the tape, stick the other end of each piece of wire to the battery in its holder (one piece of wire to each end). You have now made an electric circuit.

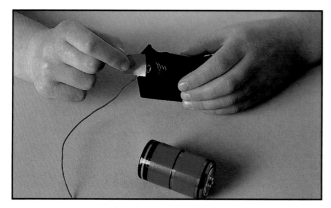

5 Does the bulb light up? Is it bright or dim? Put your light in a dark room. Does it help you to see things?

In action

The sources of light that we use to light our homes have changed throughout history, from fires and candles to gas lights and then electric lights. An English scientist called Joseph Swan invented one type of electric light bulb in 1878. The next year an American scientist called Thomas Edison invented a slightly different one. Eventually the two scientists set up a company to make electric light bulbs for people to use in their homes.

Don't stop there

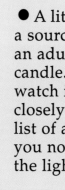

● Add another 1.5 v battery to your circuit. You will need another piece of wire as well. Make sure the second battery is connected the same way round as the first. What happens to the light now? Is it brighter or dimmer? Can you think why?

● A lit candle is also a source of light. Ask an adult to light a candle. Together watch it burn. Look closely and make a list of all the things you notice about the light.

Travelling light

LIGHT IS A TYPE OF ENERGY. It travels very, very fast. In fact nothing travels faster! It also travels in straight lines. Find out more about this here.

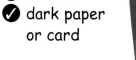
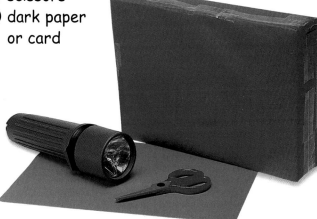

1 Turn the torch on and go into a dark room. Look closely at the light coming from the torch. Can you see the beams of light shining out from the torch into the room?

2 Ask an adult to cut a vertical slit in the box. Shine the torch through the slit. Look closely at the light that comes out of the slit.

In action

When sunlight shines through clouds or trees you can sometimes see the rays coming through the gaps. Look at the way the light rays are all in straight lines.

3 Put the box on a table and place a dark piece of paper on the table, just in front of the box. Shine the torch through the slit as before. Can you see the beam of light on the dark paper? Does it travel in a straight line?

4 What happens to the beam if you shine the torch at different angles through the slit in the box?

Keep thinking

Have you ever noticed the way bright sunlight shines into a room in rays, through the gaps in the curtains? Why do you think this is?

Don't stop there

● Make the slit in the box larger and place a large toothed comb over the hole. Shine the light through the hole. What do you notice about the way the light shines now?

● Hold up a dark piece of paper or card about 30 cm in front of your box with the slit in it and shine the torch through the slit. What can you see?

9

What does light travel through?

LIGHT TRAVELS BETTER THROUGH some materials than others. Clear materials that let all light through are called transparent. Materials that let some light through, but not all, are called translucent. Materials that light cannot travel through at all are called opaque. Find out more in this experiment.

**you will need**
- assorted pieces of fabric
- a selection of other materials (eg: a clear glass, thick card, metal tray, tissue paper, greaseproof or tracing paper, plastic bag, book, piece of wood)
- a torch

1 Look closely at the fabric and other types of materials. Predict what will happen when you shine a torch at each one. Which material will let all the light through, which just some of the light and which not any light at all?

2 Record your predictions in a table like the one above.

MATERIAL	TRANSPARENT		TRANSLUCENT		OPAQUE	
	PREDICT	RESULT	PREDICT	RESULT	PREDICT	RESULT
wood					✓	✓

3 Now shine the torch at each material. Make sure you keep the distance between the torch and the material short (about 10 cm). Get a friend to look at the other side of the material. Can they see the light shining through?

4 Record your results in the table. Now sort your materials into three groups – transparent, translucent and opaque.

Keep thinking

Have you noticed that the clouds in the sky sometimes get in the way of the Sun's rays? Do you think clouds are transparent, translucent or opaque?

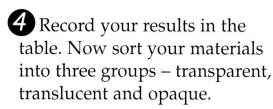

In action

Sometimes we need to use translucent or opaque materials to block out some or all of the light. Net curtains and frosted or patterned glass are used to block out some light – and also to stop people from looking in!

Blackout curtains were used in the Second World War to block out the light inside buildings completely, so that the enemy couldn't see anything to use as a target to bomb.

Don't stop there

● Take the torch around your home or school and test some other items to find materials that are either transparent, translucent or opaque.

Make a fog box

WHEN THE AIR IS CLEAR you can see through it really well. But when it gets foggy the air can be difficult to see through. As the fog gets even thicker it becomes more difficult to see things because the light does not travel well through the thick fog. Find out more in this experiment about how the thickness of a material can affect the amount of light we see.

you will need
- ✔ thin coloured card
- ✔ a shoe box
- ✔ sticky tape
- ✔ 10 clear plastic sandwich bags all cut in half
- ✔ two 1.5v batteries in battery holders
- ✔ two 2.5v bulbs in holders
- ✔ single strand wire

1 Draw a picture of the front of a car on the card and stick it inside the shoebox, on one of the small sides. Cut two holes for headlights, each just big enough for a bulb to fit through.

Keep thinking

On foggy days car drivers use special fog lights. Why do you think they use these as well as ordinary headlights?

2 Cut off the other end of the box, as shown in the picture, to make a window. Put the lid on the box.

3 Now tape each piece of plastic to the box lid so that they can be flapped over the 'window' of the box.

4 Make an electric circuit as you did on pages 6 and 7, but this time use two batteries and two bulbs. Push the two bulbs through the headlight holes. Look through the window end. Can you see the headlights?

5 Flap one layer of plastic over the window. Look through it. Can you still see the lights clearly? Add another layer. What happens? Keep adding layers. What happens to the brightness of the lights? How many layers are needed to block the lights out completely?

In action

In thick fog, bright warning lights are used on main roads to advise people to drive slowly and carefully.

When cities are very polluted, thick smog sometimes develops. Smog is a mixture of fog and smoke from factories. It can be difficult to see through, and also can cause serious health problems.

Don't stop there

● Repeat the experiment using a third 1.5v battery in the circuit. Find out if these brighter lights show up better in the plastic bag 'fog'. How many layers are needed to block the lights out now?

● On a foggy day go outside and find out which colours show up best in the fog. Do lighter colours show up better than darker ones?

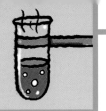

Shadow fun

IF YOU SHINE A TORCH AT AN object made of opaque material, a dark shadow is formed behind it. This is the area that the light from the torch has not reached. Shadows are also made when sunlight hits an object made of opaque material, such as your body! In fact, any light source can be used to make shadows. Find out more in this experiment.

✔ **you will need**
- ✔ thin coloured card
- ✔ sticky tape
- ✔ thin sticks or drinking straws
- ✔ a wooden frame (approx 1/2 metre square)
- ✔ a large piece of white sheet or paper
- ✔ drawing pins
- ✔ bright light source eg: spot light, slide projector or very sunny window

1 Make some rod puppets by drawing people or animals on the card. Cut them out and stick each one onto a straw or stick.

2 Make a screen with the wooden frame, white sheet and drawing pins. Stand it up and ask an adult to shine a strong light onto the back of the screen.

3 Predict where you should hold a puppet to make the best and sharpest shadow on the screen. In front of the screen or behind? Near the screen or near the light source? (Be careful, as light bulbs get very hot.) Test to find out if your predictions are correct.

4 Next hold the puppet in the best position and ask an adult to move the light nearer to the screen, then further away. What happens to the shadow?

5 Now you can use your puppets to tell a story.

 ## Don't stop there

● Paint your puppets with baby oil and then use them as shadow puppets as before. What do you notice about the shadows on the screen now? What colours are the shadows? Do you think that translucent materials can also be used to make shadows?

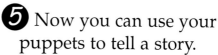 ## In action

As the position of the Sun in the sky changes throughout the day, the shadows cast by it move and change shape. Sundials use this constant movement of shadows made by sunlight to tell the time of day.

15

Bouncing light

WHEN LIGHT SHINES ON certain materials some or all of the light can 'bounce' back. This is called reflected light. Find out more about materials that reflect light in this experiment.

✓ **you will need**
- ✓ an assortment of contrasting materials (black/white; rough/smooth; shiny/dull; a mirror; metal; plastic)
- ✓ a torch
- ✓ a large piece of white card

1 Make a collection of different materials. Predict which ones will reflect the light best.

2 Now do the test, preferably in a darkened room. Shine the torch at an angle onto the material being tested. Put the card in a position to catch any reflected light. If the material reflects light well, you will see the circular shape of the torch light on the white card. Test the mirror first.

3 Now test the other materials in the same way.

4 Which materials reflected the light well? Which reflected the light best? Were the results as you predicted? Did some materials reflect no light at all? Where has the light gone?

5 Sort the materials into two groups – good and poor reflectors.

In action

Reflectors are used in many ways to keep us safe on the roads. Bicycles have special reflector lights on the back so that they can be seen easily by other road users. 'Cats' eyes'  are used in roads to help drivers see where the middle of the road is in the dark. They show up in the dark because they reflect the light coming from a car's headlights. Road signs are also often made of a reflective material.

Keep thinking

If you look into a kaleidoscope you can see interesting reflected patterns. How do you think these reflections are made?

Don't stop there

● Mirrors are good at reflecting light and making reflections. Tape two small mirrors together using masking tape. Use modelling clay to stand them up with an angle of about 60 degrees between them. Put an object in-between the mirrors. Look closely. How many reflections can you see? What happens if you move the mirrors closer together? Are there more or less reflections now? What do you think is happening?

Seeing the light!

WE SEE THINGS BECAUSE LIGHT rays coming from them enter our eyes. The rays travel through the cornea, pupil and lens and onto the retina, where they form an upside-down image. The optic nerve sends a message to the brain, which turns the image up the right way so that we can see it. Try this experiment to find out more about our eyes.

✓ **you will need**
✓ a torch
✓ a mirror
✓ a dark room

1 In a darkened room, look into the mirror to see your eyes clearly. Look closely at the black centre of each eye. This is called the pupil, a tiny hole that allows light through the eye.

2 Now shine the torch light into your eyes while you keep looking into the mirror. (Be careful – do not shine the torch into your eyes for too long!)

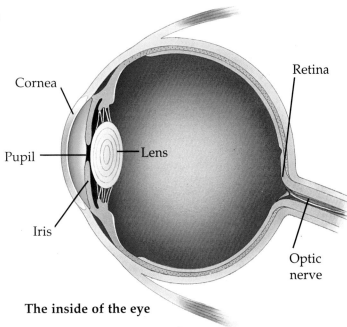

Cornea

Retina

Pupil — Lens

Iris

Optic nerve

The inside of the eye

3 Look closely to see what happens to the pupil. What did you notice? Did it change in any way?

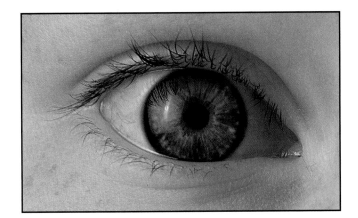

In action

Snow reflects light very well and as strong sunlight is particularly harmful to eyes, skiers wear protective goggles. This stops the glare from the light reflected off the snow from entering their eyes.

4 Keep looking in the mirror and take the torch away. Watch what happens to the pupil. Why do you think it changes?

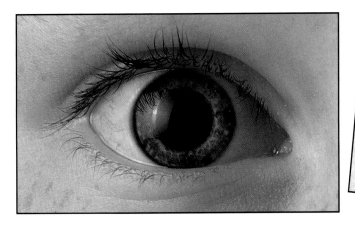

Don't stop there

● A pin-hole viewer shows the principle behind how a camera works. Make your own viewer using a card tube with tracing paper taped over one end and black paper, with a tiny pin-hole in the centre, at the other end. Hold your viewer so the pin-hole faces a sunny window and look at the tracing paper. Can you see the image of the window on the tracing paper 'screen'? Which way up is it?

Bending light – refraction

HAVE YOU NOTICED HOW PEOPLE swimming in a pool look different if you look at them when you are standing on the side? When light travelling through the air enters water at an angle, it slows down and changes direction. This is called refraction. So when we look at objects in water they look bent. Find out more in this experiment.

1 Take one of your items and slowly put it into the container while looking down at it through the water. Does it look the same as it did before? If not, what looks different?

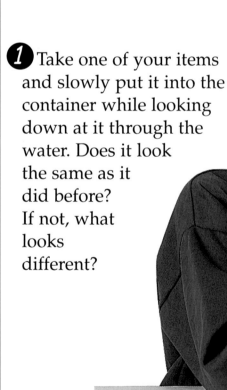

2 Now look carefully as you move the item around. What does it look like?

3 Try the experiment again using the other items. Keep a record on a simple chart of what you see each time. What do you notice?

Don't stop there

● Drop some coloured glass pebbles or beads into a clear bowl of water. Look through the side of the bowl at them. What do you notice? Still looking through the side of the bowl, try to pick them up. Which ones are easiest to pick up? Where in the bowl are the ones that are hard to pick up? Why is this?

In action

When you look into clear rock-pools the light travelling through the water to your eyes is bent. The creatures, plants, stones and shells look larger than they really are, and the pool is actually deeper than it looks.

Light and lenses

D ID YOU KNOW THAT you have a lens inside each eye to help you see? Look back at the diagram of the eye on page 18 to find out where the lens is. A lens is a transparent material that is curved on one or both sides. Some lenses are shaped to make things look bigger and some to make things look smaller.

Make your own lens in this experiment.

✔ **you will need**
- ✔ a large plastic drinks bottle
- ✔ water
- ✔ a piece of card with a simple drawing of a side view of an animal on it

1 First make your 'lens' by filling the bottle with water.

2 Stand the bottle of water on a table so you can look straight through it.

Keep thinking

In your eye, the lens makes the light bend to focus it on the back of the eye (look back at pages 18 and 19). Why do the rays of light that come out of the lens form an upside-down image on the retina? How does the way the lens works affect the way we see?

3 Hold the card with the picture on it behind the bottle and look at it through your 'lens'.

4 Move the card backwards and forwards slowly while you look through the bottle. What happens to the picture? Which way is the animal looking? Does it look bigger or smaller? Try drawing other shapes and designs on the card and experiment to see how they look through your 'lens'.

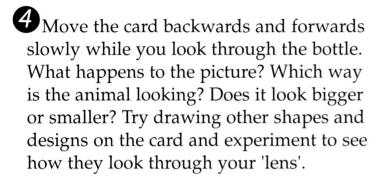

In action

Lenses come in a variety of different shapes and sizes. They are used in many different things from huge telescopes (to make far away stars and planets look bigger) to microscopes, or for the glasses or contact lenses that people wear to help them see things more clearly.

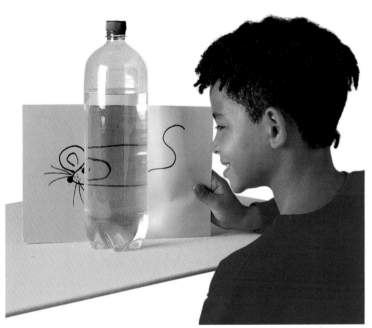

Don't stop there

● Hold a magnifying glass about two metres from a sunny window, and with your other hand hold a piece of white paper behind it. Move the paper back and forth until you can see the window image on it. Which way up is the image? Why do you think this is?

Rainbow colours

ID YOU KNOW THAT white light is really made up of many different colours, that together are known as a spectrum? You can see these colours in a rainbow. Do you think you can make white by mixing the different colours together? Find out here by using your simple circuit again from pages 6 and 7.

✓ **you will need**
- ✓ thin card
- ✓ colouring pencils or pens
- ✓ Blutack or sticky tape
- ✓ your simple circuit from pages 6 and 7 with a switch added to it
- ✓ a small motor

In action

When white light shines through a pyramid-shaped glass called a prism, the light is split into its separate colours – red, orange, yellow, green, blue, indigo and violet.

1 First cut out a circle of card about 10cm in diameter. Divide it into 7 segments.

2 Colour one segment red, the next orange, then yellow, green, blue, indigo (a blue-purple colour) and violet. This is the order of the rainbow's colours.

3 Make a small hole in the centre and fix the card onto the motor with sticky tape or Blutack.

4 Turn the switch on and look closely to see what happens to the colours on your card as they spin around. What did you see?

Don't stop there

● Look through a red, blue or green coloured filter at the room around you. Which colours look the same as usual and which ones look different? Did the colours in the room look the same through each filter?

Hidden colours

ALTHOUGH LIGHT TRAVELS in straight lines, each ray of light is made up of many waves travelling out from the source of light. The different waves in each ray of light give different colours. Sometimes the paths of the waves meet each other (this is called interference of light waves) and then we see beautiful, bright colours, as the light waves cancel out or mix with the other waves. You can see this happening in this experiment.

1 Make your wire into a 'wand' by making a loop at one end.

2 In one bowl, mix one small container full of washing-up liquid with two small containers of water. In the other bowl mix two small containers of water with two small containers of washing-up liquid.

3 Which mixture do you think will make the most colourful bubbles? Dip the wand into the first mixture and blow bubbles. Look closely at the colours. Wipe the wand clean and try making bubbles with the second mixture. Can you see the colours move and change on the surface of the bubble?

Don't stop there

● Try making bubble mixture with shampoo or shower gel. Can you make bubbles? Are they as colourful as the ones you made in the experiment?

● Carefully hold a CD disk near the light and move it around. Can you see bright, changing colours? What else can you use to achieve the same effect?

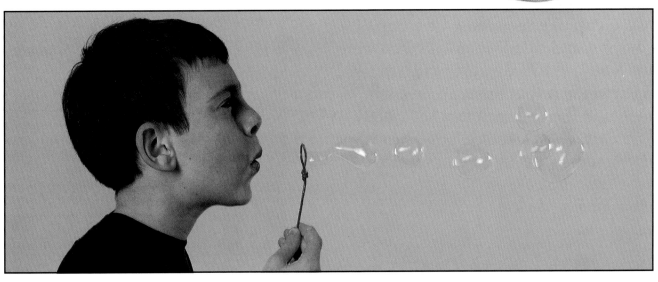

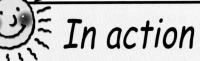 **In action**

Have you noticed the different colours that can be seen in spilt oil? This effect is caused by the interference of light waves as they bounce off the oil patch. As the rays of light cross with each other, the different colours are reflected.

Light for life

W E NEED LIGHT TO SEE things, but did you realise that other living things, like plants, need light to survive as well? Unlike us, plants are able to use light energy to make food, in a process called photosynthesis. Try this experiment to find out more.

1 Cut the feet off the pair of tights. Mix a cup of grass seed with a cup of compost and divide it equally between the feet. Use the sawdust to fill up most of the rest of the space in each foot, and then tie each foot separately with string. Make more 'grass heads' in the same way and if you want try growing some of them upside down!

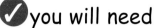
✔ you will need
- ✔ a pair of tights
- ✔ grass seed
- ✔ sawdust
- ✔ scraps of fabric and permanent marker pens for decorating
- ✔ water-proof glue
- ✔ compost
- ✔ string

2 Make a face on each grass head using scraps of fabric and pens.

💡 Keep thinking

Too much sunlight can be dangerous for people! Strong sunlight can burn our skin and sometimes causes skin cancer. What can you do to protect yourself from the Sun? If the Sun stopped shining, how do you think it would affect you?

3 Stand the heads in water and put them near a bright window until you see the shoots begin to show. Remember to keep them damp.

4 Put one head in a dark cupboard and leave the other in the light. If you have made extra grass heads, put them in various light or dark places around the house. Water all the grass heads regularly and look closely to see how they grow (leave them for about two weeks). What do you notice?

Don't stop there

● What do you think will happen to the grass heads if you swap them, and put the one from the light in the dark and vice versa? Try it. Water them as before, leave them both for about a week and watch to see what happens. What is the main change?

In action

The Sun's light energy is so powerful that it can be harnessed and used to make electricity. This is called solar power. The energy is 'collected' by using mirrors to reflect the sunlight onto a receiver, where it is converted into electricity.

Glossary

This glossary gives the meaning of each word as it is used in this book

Air An invisible mixture of gases, mainly nitrogen and oxygen, that surrounds the Earth.
Artificial Not natural. Made by people.

Battery A device that stores and produces electricity.

Candle A source of light made of wax with a central wick. When the wick is lit it gives off heat and light.
Cat's eyes Guiding lights in the centre of some roads. They contain mirrors to reflect light from car headlights, so that drivers can see the centre of the road at night.
Coloured filter A transparent sheet of coloured material.

Electric circuit The path that electricity takes.
Electricity A type of energy which can be used to make light, to heat things and to make machines work.

Focus To adjust light to get a clear and sharp picture.

Gas A gas, such as air, has no fixed shape or volume. It spreads out to fill the container. Often you cannot see a gas.

Harness To use the energy from natural resources such as water or sunlight.

Image The 'picture' formed when light travels though a lens.
Interference When waves of light meet each other.

Kaleidoscope A tube with mirrors inside that you look down to see changing patterns.

Lens Transparent material specially shaped to bend light rays in a particular way.

Machine A device, such as a lever, that makes it easier to do a task.
Magnify Make bigger.
Mains electricity Very powerful electric current supplied to our homes.
Materials Everything! All solids, liquids and gases are materials, not just fabrics.
Microscope An instrument for magnifying tiny objects. It uses lenses to do this.
Mist Very small drops of water vapour in the air.
Moon Our Moon is a natural satellite that orbits (circles) the Earth.

Natural From nature, not made by people.

Opaque Does not allow light to pass through it.

Optic nerve The name of the nerve that goes from the eye to the brain.

Photosynthesis The process used by plants to convert light energy into food.

Pin-hole viewer A box with a pin-hole at one end and a 'screen' at the other, used to show how a camera works.

Pollution Harmful substances sometimes mixed with the air or in water.

Prism A solid piece of transparent glass or plastic (often looking like a pyramid) that can be used to split up white light into its colours.

Pupil A small hole in the iris (the coloured part of the eye around the pupil) that lets light into the eye.

Rainbow The spectrum visible in the sky when light shines through raindrops.

Rays Thin lines of light.

Reflected Light is reflected when it is bounced off a surface.

Refraction A process in which the path of a light ray is bent (changes direction) as it passes from one material to another.

Retina The back of the inside of the eyeball where an image forms.

Shadow A dark area caused when light rays are blocked by an opaque object.

Solar power The use of energy from sunlight.

Sources of light Things which make light are called primary sources of light. Things that reflect light are called secondary sources of light.

Spectrum The seven different colours that together make white light.

Sun The Sun is our nearest star and is seen as a yellow-orange ball in the daytime. You must never look directly at the Sun because it can damage your eyes.

Sundials One of the earliest ways to tell the time, made from a pointer on a dial which casts a shadow to show the changing position of the Sun as it appears to move across the sky throughout the day.

Telescope A machine, containing lenses, used to see far away objects more clearly.

Translucent Allowing some light, but not much, to pass through.

Transparent Completely see-through.

Index